MILITARY VEHICLES

THE MARSHALL CAVENDISH
ILLUSTRATED GUIDE TO
MILITARY
VEHICLES

Christopher Chant

Illustrated by John Batchelor

Marshall Cavendish
New York · London · Toronto · Sydney

Library Edition 1989

© Marshall Cavendish Limited 1989
© DPM Services Limited 1989

Published by Marshall Cavendish Corporation
147 West Merrick Road
Freeport
Long Island
N.Y. 11520

Produced by DPM Services Limited
Designed by Graham Beehag
Illustrations © John Batchelor

Library of Congress Cataloging-in-Publication Data

Chant, Christopher.
  Military vehicles/written by Chris Chant: Illustrated by John
Batchelor.
      p.   cm−(The Marshall Cavendish illustrated guides)
  Includes index.
  Summary: Provides an illustrated history of military land vehicles
and describes how they operate.
  ISBN 1-85435-090-0
  1. Armored vehicles, Military−Juvenile literature. [1. Armored
vehicles, Military.] I. Batchelor, John H., [1]. II. Title.
III. Series: Chant, Christopher. Marshall Cavendish illustrated
guides.
UG446.5.C4625 1989
358'.18−dc19   88-28705
                                                        CIP
                                                         AC

    ISBN 1-85435-085-4 (set).

Printed and bound in Italy by L.E.G.O. SpA, Vicenza

Throughout history, the armies of the world have needed some form of transport: vehicles for the movement of men and equipment rather than for fighting. From earliest times to the beginning of present century, armies tried to live off the land in which they were operating, but still needed transport vehicles for the movement of heavy equipment, additional food supplies, ammunition and, in all too many cases, the offiers' baggage and furniture. Hand carts provided a measure of transport capability, though they meant that tired troops were faced with the problem of pulling their own equipment and so becoming still more tired. More effective by far were animal-drawn wagons: oxen were used for the large wagons carrying heavy equipment, but were very slow, while horses and mules provided slightly greater speed, but lower power. Generals tried to have their animals, like their men, live off the land, but this was seldom possible in campaign lasting more than a few weeks, and the result was that much of the available transport had to

A French field ambulance of World War I. These vehicles could not move close to the tortured front-line areas, but were literally vital in moving casualties from rear-area stations to base hospitals.

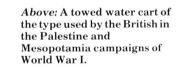

Above: A towed water cart of the type used by the British in the Palestine and Mesopotamia campaigns of World War I.

Right: Part of a British pontoon bridging train of World War I, each cart carrying one pontoon, its anchor and sufficient bridging material to tie the pontoon to its neighbor.

be allocated to the movement of fodder to keep the rest of the transport train moving! One positive side to the use of animal transport, however, was the possibility of using the animals for food if the supply situation became impossible.

Well-conducted armies tried to keep non-essential elements to a minimum to avoid overwhelming their limited transport services, but there are many examples of armies in which the men had to go short of food, medicine, ammunition, or other vital supplies because the available transport had been commandeered for the comforts and even the families of the officer corps.

The science of keeping troops supplied in the field is called logistics, and in various periods of history, logistics have been a highly developed and highly significant science, allowing the great generals to make best use of relatively small forces to inflict crushing defeats on

Built in large numbers from 1942 and often known as the "Beep," the T214 four-wheel drive truck was built by Dodge in the U.S. and in modified form in Canada. The type had a 92-bhp engine of 230 cu.in., and could carry three-quarters of a ton of payload at 55 mph.

their enemies through a combination of mobility and good physical condition. Logistics were, of course, aided by the development of good road systems, and a major boost was provided by the development of railroads. The latter provided the chance for large quantities of men and material to be moved long distances at high speed, and the effect of the railroads on military thinking were felt as early as the Civil War (1861-1865) and the Franco-Prussian War (1870-1871). The nations of the European mainland were aware from an early date of the effect that railroads could have on Europeans wars, and their governments thus moved readily into the control of how their national railroad networks spread: private enterprise was welcomed as a means of offsetting cost, but the governments made sure that national military and economic interests were

served in the creation of new routes. The Germans raised the science of rail mobility to its peak in the period up to the outbreak of World War I in 1914.

Japan's strategic plan in the Russo-Japanese War (1904-1905) was based on the defeat of the Russian forces in Korea and Manchuria before large-scale reinforcements could reach them along the Trans-Siberian Railroad from western Russia. Japan's planners

The British provided their heavy artillery with a measure, but only a small measure, of mobility by using traction engines. This is a Daimler-Foster tractor with a 105-hp Daimler petrol engine used to tow a 15-in howitzer.

appreciated that their army was completely outnumbered by that of imperial Russia, but saw that the relatively small forces in the Russian Far Eastern provinces could be outnumbered and defeated before sizeable numbers of Russia's 4.5 million soldiers could be moved by the long, single-track railroad to help their comrades in the Far East. And so it proved.

While the railroads completely changed the nature of military transport in the regions behind the battle area and so forced changes in the period's strategic doc-

Below: **Even with the advent of powered trucks as a major force in World War I, there was still vast scope for animal-drawn transport, and also for derivatives of such transport for towing behind powered vehicles.**

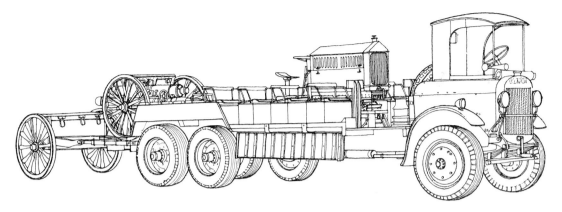

Above: Motor transport opened up the possibility of greater mobility for artillery by making the whole equipment truck-borne rather than just truck-towed.

trines of how to wage war as a whole, they could not move equipment right to the men in the front line. In this tactical situation of how to fight individual battles, animal transport was still the only effective means of transport. Supplies were moved by rail to massive dumps set up at the railheads as close as possible to the front line, and then collected by animal transport columns for onward movement to the fighting men. The railroads could also deliver additional men, but once they had reached the railhead, the only means of

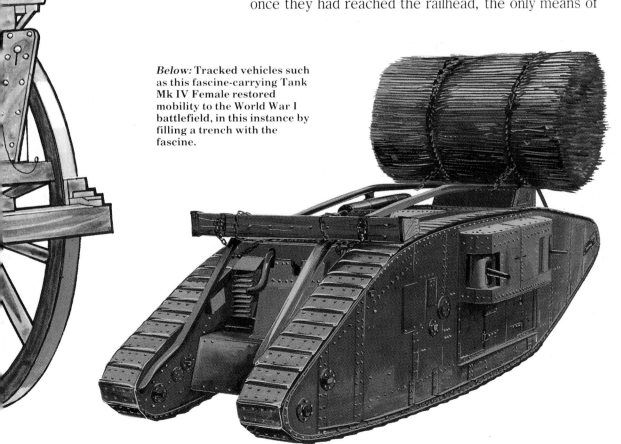

Below: Tracked vehicles such as this fascine-carrying Tank Mk IV Female restored mobility to the World War I battlefield, in this instance by filling a trench with the fascine.

movement to the front was still the soldier's age-old standby: his feet.

Change had been in the air, though, since the development of the automotive steam engine and later of the internal combustion engine. Once the steam engine had been developed for railroad use as the steam locomotive, it was only a comparatively short step to

A German Bussing mobile workshop of World War I. The sides are shown in their lowered positions, where they served as working platforms.

its use as road equipment in the steam traction engine. This in fact found its most useful employment as a farm tractor, but was also used on roads for the movement of heavy loads. The weight of the traction engine was a hindrance to agility and speed, but provided excellent towing capabilities, which prompted army officers to consider the type as a heavy gun tractor. The Indus-

One of the oddest military vehicles of World War II was the British Army's Crossley IGL8 searchlight vehicle. Carried on a six-wheel truck with four-wheel drive, it resembled a conventional truck until the tarpaulin and supporting bows were removed from the flatbed to reveal a 36-inch searchlight powered by its own 24-kW generator.

trial Revolution, which had allowed the development of powerful steam engines, had also permitted the creation of heavy artillery able to fire enormous shells over great ranges, but their pieces of ordnance were all but impossible to move even with large teams of horses or oxen. When the guns were emplaced, they could only be used to good effect if they could be fed with constantly renewed supply of ammunition. The traction engine was adopted to this task, for it had adequate pulling strength even off roads to tow heavy artillery and the limbers for the ammunition. The traction engine was inevitably slow, and therefore something of a tactical liability, but officers reasoned that heavy artillery was unlikely to have to decamp in a great hurry. Since heavy artillery was used only in limited quantities up to the beginning of World War I, the numbers of traction engines bought were comparatively small.

But traction engines were in themselves something of an evolutionary dead end, because even in their

A Minerva armored car, a touring automobile fitted with armor plate and armed with an 8-mm Hotchkiss machine-gun.

A Rolls-Royce armored car of the type used by the British in North Africa and the Middle East from World War I right into World War II.

fully-developed forms, they were limited by their considerable size, ponderous performance, and need for large quantities of coal and water. In the last 15 years of the 19th century, the internal combustion engine made great developmental strides from its very simple and limited beginnings to the stage where useful power and adequate reliability were well within sight. By comparison with the steam engine, the internal combustion engine offered a far superior power-to-weight ratio, while demanding less in terms of fuel and water.

Many of the world's armies had moved into mechanization before World War I, but their main transport requirements were still met by animals. The effect of this reliance was felt in the first days of the war. Germany's strategic scheme was the "Schlieffen Plan," calling for the right wing of Germany's advancing armies to sweep around to the west of the French capital, Paris, before turning south and then east to trap the Allied armies. But the distance was just too

A Parisian taxi cab of the period leading up to World War I. As the Germans were halted just outside Paris in September 1914, such cabs were used to rush fresh men to the front along the Marne River.

The longest military vehicle ever designed was the U.S. Army's experimental 572-ft. Overland Train built in the early 1960s by R. G. LeTourneau, Inc. The type has 4,680 shp for maximum speed of 20 mph at a weight of 400 tons, and control of the 54-wheel vehicle needed a crew of six.

great for the German right wing army, which was exhausted and had to turn before reaching Paris. This retreat resulted in Germany's first defeat of the war at the first Battle of the Marne, in which the Allies made extensive use of motor transport (including English buses and Parisian taxicabs) to ferry fresh reinforcements to the battlefront.

After this, each side tried unsuccessfully to outflank the other to the north, this so-called "race to the sea" resulting in the creation of the unmoving front line between the English Channel coast and the Swiss frontier that dominated the rest of the war. The front line was fortified on each side with semi-permanent trench lines, barbed wire, and machine gun positions.

A Rolls-Royce armored car in conditions typical of those in North Africa and the Middle East, where one of the type's great virtues was reliability.

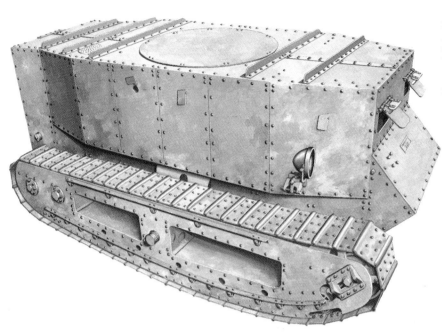

Left: The British "Little Willie" of 1915 was a prototype tank, but with its low tracks and provision for a central turret, it was prophetic of later tanks rather than typical of World War I thinking.

Right: The Steyr-Daimler-Puch 1500 A was the German army's standard 1.5-ton truck in World War II. The design was by Dr. Ferdinand Porsche, and all four wheels were driven.

Farther back from the front line, each side built up great stocks of the artillery which the generals saw as the only means to defeat the enemy's artillery and destroy the barbed wire and machine gun defenses of the front line. Then, the generals hoped, the infantry could storm through the enemy's front line defenses and create a gap through which horse cavalry could pour and inflict a war-winning defeat.

It did not happen, and with hindsight, it is possible to see that it could never have happened with the transport and concepts available in the first part of World War I. The war stagnated. Vast offensives gained the

Above: A British experimental vehicle was this Armstrong Siddeley B10 tractor, an articulated type with eight-wheel drive.

victor a few hundred yards at the cost of hundreds of thousands of men. Even in this grim scenario, transport had its part to play. The front-line soldiers were served by foot or at best by animal transport, but slightly farther behind the front, there buzzed increasingly large fleets of motorcycles for dispatch riders, ambulances, supply trucks, staff cars, and specialized vehicles. These last became enormously important in the course of the "Great War," offering unglamorous, but absolutely vital, services such as water purification and delousing, and all manner of repair facilities. Trucks were also used on an increasing scale to ferry ammunition to the gun lines, though the static nature of the war also meant that the larger guns could be served by small railroads laid especially for the purpose.

The same pattern of static warfare was followed on other fronts such as those in Italy between the Italians and the Austro-Hungarians; in the Dardanelles (Gallipoli) between the Turks and the Allies (Australians, British, and New Zealanders), and in the Balkans between the Bulgarians and the Allies. Operations of more mobile nature developed on the Eastern Front between the Russians and the Central Powers (Ger-

Right: A British AEC Matador tractor used its four-wheel drive and forward winch to pull itself and the 5.5-in gun howitzer up the bank of the Weser River after crossing a U.S. army pontoon bridge in 1945.

many and Austria-Hungary); in the Middle East between the Turks and the British; and in East Africa between the Germans and the various Allied nations. Some motor transport was used on the Eastern Front, but here the mainstays were draft animals and marching men. The East Africa campaign was one of marching infantry with comparatively small numbers of animals, but the Middle Eastern campaigns of Mesopotamia and Palestine saw more extensive use of motor transport. There was still extensive use of animals in both their draft and ridden forms (the latter including camels as well as horses and mules,) but mechanized vehicles played an increasingly important part in mobile operations and prophesied the way mobile operations would develop in World War II. Long, enveloping movements were made to cut off and trap the Turkish armies; infantry was carried in trucks and supported by truck-drawn artillery, while armored cars were used for deep reconnaissance and for attacks on the Turks' rear areas and lines of communication. Undertaken in the heat, dust, and difficult terrain of the Middle East,

Typical of the type of commercial chassis adapted for staff use by the military in the 1920s was the Adler "3 Gd," known in service with the German army as the Kfz ll. This was very similar to the 60-bhp civilian model, but had larger tires, a revised rear-axle ratio for better performance in adverse conditions, and canvas curtains over the door openings.

During World War II, the need
to carry out engineer
operations in combat areas
led to the rapid development
of armored engineer vehicles
such as this Caterpillar
heavy-duty dozer.

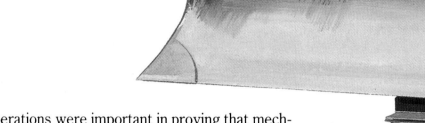

these operations were important in proving that mechanized vehicles could cope with the extreme conditions
of war.

Mechanization also reached the Western Front in
France during 1916 in the form of the tank, but these
fall outside the scope of this book. In 1918, the final
Allied victory was at last ensured by the British victory
in the Battle of Amiens (August 8, 1918,) but the
breakthrough made possible by this success was ex-
ploited by the conventional transport of the Western
Front rather than by masses of motor transport.

In the years immediately after World War I, the
countries that had formed the Allied team were too
exhausted, both spiritually and financially, to attempt
any but the most superficial development of ideas
proved useful in the "Great War." During the course of
the late 1920s and early 1930s, the more far-sighted
armies decided that full mechanization was the true

path forward in purely military terms: the two most significant were the American and British armies, which launched ambitious schemes to replace all their animals, with the very limited exception of mules in such specialized tasks as jungle and mountain warfare. Henceforward, it was planned, the infantry would ride in trucks or, in the case of American soldiers in the

battle zone, in half-tracked armored personnel carriers that combined the advantages of the truck in terms of cheapness and simplicity with the cross-country mobility of the tracked vehicle. Trucks were improved in their size, load-carrying capability, reliability, and versatility with more powerful engines, more flexible transmissions, and drive to all four or six wheels for better mobility in true cross-country operations; and considerable ingenuity went into the creation of truck-mounted services that could follow the infantry and satisfy all their battlefield needs.

It was planned that the motorized or mechanized infantry should operate with armored forces to create combined-arms teams. The motorized infantry was to be carried in trucks and supported by light and medium artillery of the truck-towed type, while the mechanized infantry was to be carried in armored personnel carriers and supported by light and medium artillery of the self-propelled type mounted on a tracked chassis. The British and Soviets led the way with the creation of motorized infantry, while the American forces were more ambitious and pushed forward with the creation of mechanized infantry.

This reflected industrial capability in addition to mili-

Above: An experimental Crossley tractor tested by the British with Kegresse half-tracks.

Below: A British medium tank of World War I, based on a Daimler automobile chassis.

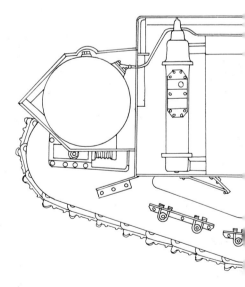

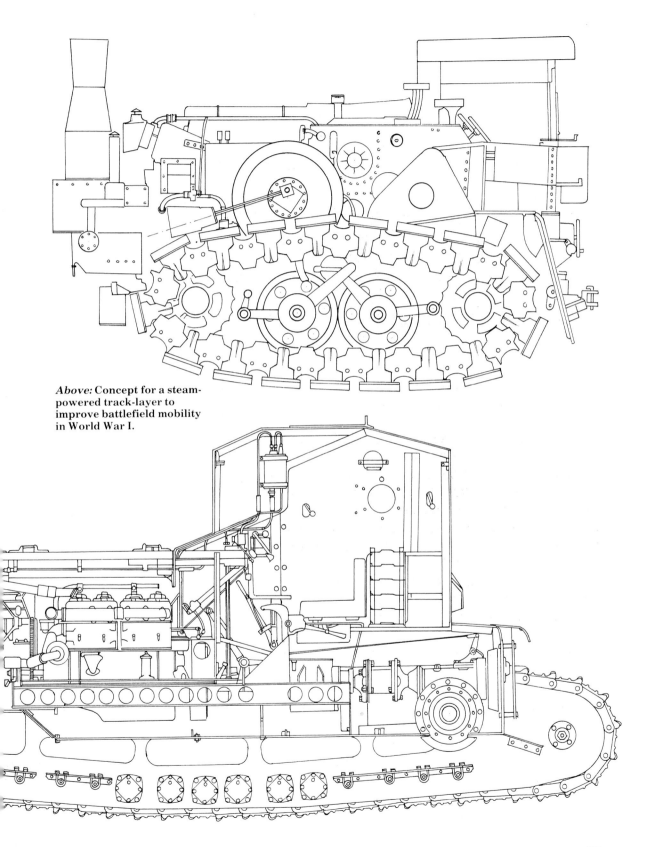

Above: Concept for a steam-powered track-layer to improve battlefield mobility in World War I.

The German equivalent of the U.S. Jeep in World War II was the excellent Kubelwagen, based on the Volkswagen automobile and here fitted with the optional propeller/rudder unit driven by the standard engine to provide amphibious capability.

tary thinking. The British and Soviets had fairly well advanced truck industries that could turn their attention without undue cost or delay to highly reliable load-carriers with adequate cross-country performance. The Americans, on the other hand, saw the advantages of using their dynamic truck industry to create for the mechanized infantry the more expensive personnel carriers that provided superior cross-country mobility as well as protection for the embarked infantry.

The Americans were fortunate that World War II was two years further away from them than for the European nations; the delay allowed the development and production of the classic M2 and M3 series of half-track carriers that were developed into a host of unarmed and armed forms in the war, and which have been kept in service by a number of armies right up to the present.

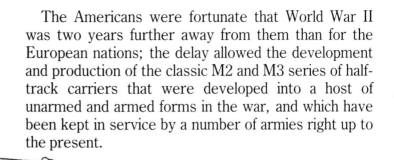

Above: To "amphibianize" tanks the British used this Duplex Drive with propellers and a canvas flotation screen.

Above right: A Morris 15-cwt truck with four-wheel drive as a tanker.

Right: A mobile workshop based on the M&B truck.

Oddly enough, given their successes in the first campaigns of World War II, the Germans were not as highly motorized or mechanized as most of their adversaries. The success of the Germans' *Blitzkrieg* tactics against Poland, the Low Countries and France, Yugoslavia, Greece and, initially, the U.S.S.R. has produced the legend that masses of German tanks thundered forward with hordes of motorized and/or mechanized infantry, supported by truck-towed artillery. This was not the case, for the Germans were late into the field of army mechanization, and until 1941, were still reliant mainly on draft animals. The Panzer divisions

Vehicles typical of the German situation in 1944 and 1945: from left to right these are a heavy assault gun, a Steyr-Daimler-Puch 1500 A 1.5-tonne truck and an SdKfz 6/1 half-track used for tasks as different as troop movement and artillery towing.

A trim little German vehicle of World War II was the Kleines Kettenkrad (SdKfz 2), a hybrid that was in effect a tricycle with a single wheel at the front and twin tracks at the rear. Powered by a 36-hp engine, this "motorcycle" was designed as an air portable tractor for the German airborne army's light guns. In addition to the driver, it could carry two men facing backward.

were supported by artillery, sometimes towed by trucks or, in the case of heavier equipment, tracked tow vehicles rather than draft animals. But they were very poorly supported by the infantry, which generally had to march. So, the German victories were good ideas turned into brilliant practice, and a careful reading of World War II history reveals that the German plans frequently came close to disaster when the Panzer divisions outpaced the weary infantry divisions and then had to wait in dangerously exposed positions for the support to catch up!

On the Allied side, especially in the American camp, World War II saw the real blossoming of military transport. From 1943 onward, the Allied advances relied ever more heavily on tracked and wheeled vehicles for the supplies and the mobility that enabled them to grind down the Germans' still formidable fighting machine. As in World War I, there were vehicles for all purposes, but the availability of more and better vehicles allowed ingenious military planners to come

A British folding motorcycle designed for use by airborne units.

Above: **The Dodge T215 was used by the U.S. Army for reconnaissance and command purposes.**

Below: **The Carden-Loyd Mk V was a British 1926 effort to combine wheels and tracks to produce an effective machine-gun carrier.**

up with more and more types of specialized vehicles to ease the task of the fighting men. There were, of course, the standard types, such as motorcycles for the urgent movement of messages when radio or telephone communication could not be ensured or trusted, supply trucks, artillery tractors, ambulances, staff cars, and the like. But in addition to the half-track already mentioned (a type that was also used by the

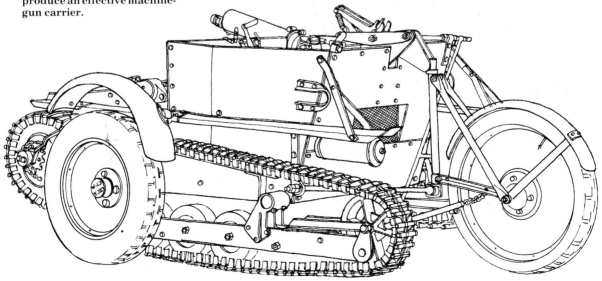

A Chevrolet truck used by the British Long-Range Desert Group with heavy armament, sand channels, and extra water and fuel.

Germans to a smaller extent), World War II saw the widespread adoption of vehicles such as the jeep, DUKW, amphibious tractor (often called amtrack or amphtrack), tank transporter, and many others for a host of particular tasks that were not in themselves absolutely vital, but which taken together made the Allied victory possible. As Winston Churchill put it, "Victory is the beautiful bright-colored flower; transport is the stem, without which it could never have blossomed."

It is impossible to overstate the importance of the Willys Jeep, whose name has become current in modern language as just the jeep. This was (and in its more modern versions continues to be) an exceptional little vehicle of sturdy construction. Its one real problem was the poor protection offered to the crew in bad weather; but in all military respects, the jeep was superb, with a rugged engine, four-wheel drive, and a high ground-clearance to provide a good combination of road and cross-country performance with the ability to ford modestly deep streams without preparation. These are the hallmarks of the true military transport,

and the jeep had them all in good measure despite its small overall size. The jeep was used for all manner of tasks, ranging from communications to front-line supply and casualty evacuation, to scouting. Other nations had their equivalents, but that which came closest in performance and capability to the American vehicles was the Germans' Kubelwagen, based on the chassis and automotive system of the Volkswagen. But the Germans could never match the Americans for production, so their Kubelwagen was less important in overall terms. American production was vast, allowing the jeep to be issued on a lavish scale to U.S. forces, and on almost as generous a scale to many of the Allied forces.

Above: Another combat variant of the tank was the armored bridgelayer such as this Canadian development of the British Churchill tank, and known as the Mk II SBG AVRE (Standard Box Girder, Armoured Vehicle Royal Engineers).

The DUKW (pronounced 'duck') was designed in 1942 by General Motors in collaboration with the yacht designers Sparkman & Stevens as an amphibious truck suitable for amphibious operations. The DUKW could be driven into the water from ramp-equipped ships or lowered by crane, thereafter shuttling between ships and inland dumps with 5,000 pounds of supplies or 25 troops. The DUKW was liable to swamping in all but calm water, but proved itself to be of immense value in amphibious operations, such as those which took the Allied armies ashore in Italy and France; and they played a prominent part in major river-crossing operations, such as that to ferry the Allies across the River Rhine and into the heart of Germany in April, 1945. In the water, the DUKW was steered by a rudder and

The Allies' most important amphibious truck in the European theater was the DUKW, a 2.5-ton vehicle with drive-wheel drive, supplemented by its propeller and rudder for waterborne movement at 5.5 knots in good conditions. The type could carry 25 troops or 5,000 lb of freight.

driven by its propeller at 5.5 knots; on land, it became a conventional six-wheel drive vehicle with a maximum speed of 50 mph. Other nations attempted similar vehicles, but none was as successful as the DUKW.

The amphibious tractor was more properly called the Landing Vehicle Tracked, and was designed to provide much the same capability as the DUKW, with the added advantage of cleated tracks that provided waterborne propulsion as well as a superior ability to climb over reefs and up difficult shores. The LVT underwent intensive development in World War II, and was successively fitted with features such as a ramp so that it could be used to land troops for assault landings, armor protection, machine gun armament and, in later models, offensive armament in the form of a light tank turret or a 75-mm howitzer. Production was extensive, and the importance of the type to the American effort against the Japanese in the Pacific was enormous. The type was also used in Europe against the Germans, and as with the DUKW, there were never enough to meet demand.

The Allies' extensive employment of amphibious assault operations also demanded the creation of specialized vehicles such as beach armored recovery

More capable than the DUKW, and used mostly in the Pacific theater, was the LVT (Landing Vehicle Tracked). This is an early LVT 1, with cleated tracks to provide waterborne propulsion.

vehicles, which were tanks stripped of their armament and fitted with deep wading equipment to allow their use as wreckers on crowded beaches where bogged down or disabled vehicles could cause a disastrous delay in the flow of men and equipment off the assault beach.

The role of the tank transporter is self-evident. It was designed for the rapid and long-distance movement of tanks, so that the short-lived tracks on the tanks would not be unduly worn by slowing churning along roads and across country. The availability of tank transporters also allowed the tank forces greater operational mobility, allowing substantial armored forces to

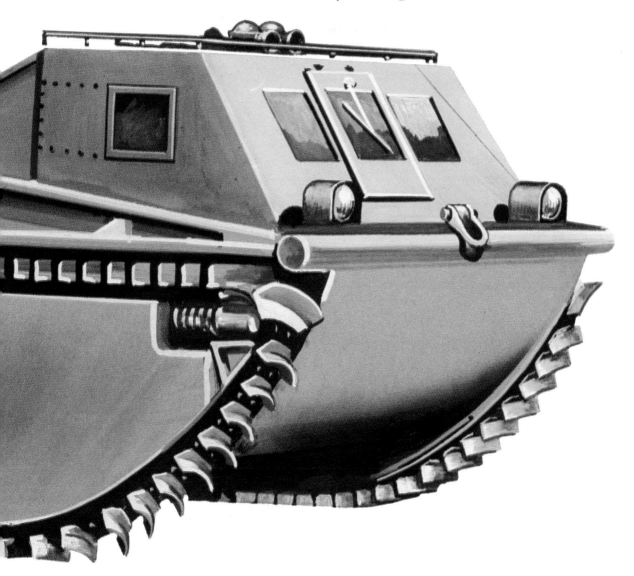

Above: Operations in remoter areas called for ingenuity as well as skill, as shown by this improvised raft to ferry a light truck across a Hong Kong river.

Above left: A Guy ANT infantry truck of the British in World War II.

Left: The Dodge T214 weapons carrier was a utility truck with four-wheel drive.

appear where the enemy least expected them in the peak of physical condition.

Other types were developed and placed into service in smaller numbers, but their importance was still great. It is vehicles of this type that have become more important in the period since World War II; typical are bulldozers and combat engineer tractors. In World War II, many tanks, especially of the older types that were approaching obsolescence in their primary gun tank role, were fitted with a hydraulically operated bulldozer blade that allowed their use for the creation of beach and river bank gradients suitable for other heavy vehicles, the creation of level positions for the artillery, and the quick creation of dirt barriers. Military conversions of civilian bulldozers were also used, and both types have been further developed since World War II. The tank fitted with a blade does not

The U.S. Army has been a firm
believer in mechanization for
most of this century, and its
World War II forces were very
well provided with trucks for
basic movement and supply,
this GMC vehicle being
typical.

Germany's largest tractor of World War II was the Schwerer Zugkraftwagen 18t (SdKfz 9), a 17.7-ton half-track powered by a 250-bhp gasoline engine for a maximum speed of 31 mph. In addition to the driver, the vehicle accommodated eight men on open bench seats, and while designed as a tank recovery vehicle, it was later adopted as a super-heavy artillery tractor. The 81.7-ton Kanone 3, a 9.45-inch artillery equipment, could be broken down into five components towed by SdKfz 9 vehicles.

The British Ark type of ramp bridging tank was developed in World War II to drive into a gap and then extend its fore-and-aft bridging sections so that other vehicles could drive over the top. This is an Ark based on the Churchill infantry tank.

lose much in mobility or speed, but can quickly create for itself a dug-in position that leaves only the turret and its main gun exposed to enemy view and therefore enemy attack. Proper bulldozers provide the same capability as their World War II forerunners, but with greater speed and agility. From these two basic types evolved the combat engineer tractor, designed to undertake these and other more warlike roles in a vehicle fitted with specialist equipment (an earth auger, bulldozer blade, winch, jib crane, and demolition gun). To provide maximum protection for the crew, these combat engineer tractors are almost always

The U.S. forces' latest "jeep" is the LTV "Hummer," a four-wheel drive vehicle adopted in 1983 for mass production in a number of forms with a 130-bhp diesel engine.

The White M3 was the classic half-track of World War II, and is still in widespread service to this day. The front-mounted roller helps the vehicle to rise out of ditches and the like.

The combination of a gun and a tracked chassis produces a vehicle known as a self-propelled gun. This provides a high level of mobility, though battlefield survival is enhanced in later vehicles by the use of a firing cab enclosed by armor.

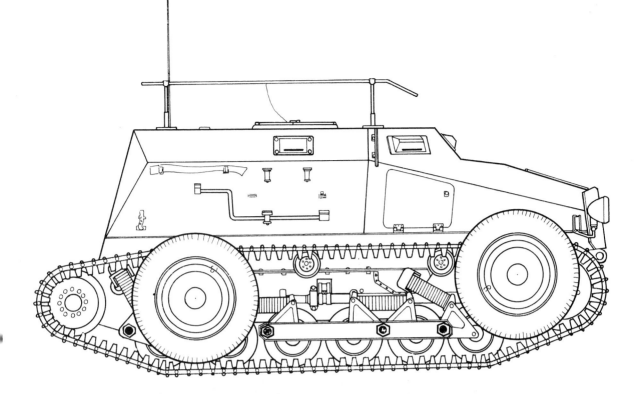

Above: Over the years many nations have sought to combine wheels and tracks on a single vehicle, the former being lowered for high-speed road travel, and then raised to permit the tracks to take over for cross-country movement.

Light weight and tactical versatility are the trademarks of modern military vehicles, and this certainly applies to the Willys "Military Mule," which is little more than a 925-pound platform with four-wheel drive from a 17-bhp engine, an exposed driver's position at the front, and an unobstructed flatbed behind it.

Left: A Chevrolet C60L truck chassis and cab fitted with a house-type office body.

Left: A Bantam 40 BRC in service with the British 6th Armoured Division.

Above: The Jeep was as important to Allied victory as any weapon.

Below: A Mack NR9 10-tonner loading with supplies at Antwerp.

Obsolete chassis are often
used as the basis of support
vehicles: this is a British Bren
Gun Carrier in service as a
pontoon transport before the
Allies' Rhine crossings of
1945.

based on the chassis and hull of main battle tanks, which also gives them much the same performance as the tank forces they are designed to support.

Since World War II, there have appeared no radically new military transport concepts. Emphasis has been placed on developing the notions explored and proved in World War II. The global nature of modern warfare, for example, had resulted in the development of freight and personnel transports suitable for use in a wide variety of climate and terrain. At the same time, however, the needs of the most extreme conditions have been met by the creation of highly specialized types such as snowmobiles and swamp-crossers: the former are in fairly extensive service, but the latter are still largely experimental.

Mobility for wheeled vehicles has been provided in a number of ways, one concept being the articulated chassis as used in the LTV-built "Gama Goat," designed by R. Gamaunt of California. It has a 103-bhp engine and full six-wheel drive for a two-wheel forward section and four-wheel rear unit.

Modern military vehicles are mechanically more advanced than the vehicles of World War II, with features such as automatic transmission and high-technology suspension. The gasoline engine has given way almost completely to the diesel with its more readily available fuel, lower risk of fire, and higher range for a given volume of fuel. Complementing this internal development are three external tendencies that are more readily apparent in the development of modern military transport: tactical versatility, enclosed accommodation (to provide protection against nuclear, biological, and chemical warfare agents), and measures to improve cross-country mobility.

Tactical versatility has been enhanced by basing modern transports on a modular core, namely a core chassis and automotive system that can be built up as several types of specialized vehicle, or alternatively fitted with a flatbed onto which can be lowered a palletized or containerized system that fits the vehicle to the desired role. For example, palletized freight can be moved on one trip, and then the vehicle's flatbed can be fitted with a containerized communications system with its own power supply to provide a unit with good communications.

This also fits with the tendency toward enclosed accommodation as a measure against some of the effects of N.B.C. warfare. Filters are used to remove harmful agents, and the accommodation also provides air-conditioning and temperature control in addition to protection, which helps to keep the embarked personnel as fresh as possible.

Mobility has been increased in both wheeled and

The M113 is the U.S. Army's current mainstay in the armored personnel carrier role.

tracked transports. In more advanced armies, there has been a move toward comparatively light aluminum bodies on fully tracked vehicles with their inherently superior cross-country mobility, but there has also been considerable development of six- and eight-wheel drive wheeled vehicles whose mobility is not completely inferior to that of tracked vehicles, but which are much cheaper to develop and produce, and also considerably easier to maintain. These last are of great importance to the developing countries that are the main market for these wheeled vehicles. It is hard to see that there are in the short term any more roles that can be undertaken by military transports, but the future will certainly see further improvement in performance and mobility.

Modern successor to the Jeep is the LTV (American Motors General) "Hummer," known more formally as the HMMWV or High-Mobility Multi-Purpose Wheeled Vehicle.

Glossary

Amphtrack (or amtrack):   amphibious freight/troop transport, generally based on an armored and tracked chassis

Armored personnel carrier: battlefield troop transport (generally tracked or half-tracked) providing its embarked men with a measure of armor protection

Draft animal: animal used for movement of equipment and supplies rather than for riding

Fodder: foodstuffs required for animals

Half-track: vehicle with forward steering wheels and rear-mounted track units, conferring much improved cross-country performance than that possible with wheels only

Logistics: the art (and also the science) of keeping troops supplied with all their essential needs in terms of food, medicines, ammunition etc.

Mechanized infantry: infantry carried in armored personnel carriers

Mobility: the term used in military affairs to describe the ability of troops to move quickly and effectively from one point to another as demanded by the tactical situation

Motorized infantry: infantry carried in trucks

Railhead: the end of a railroad nearest any desired spot

Strategy: that part of the military art concerned with the winning of wars by success in a series of battles

Tactics: that part of the military art concerned with winning battles

Traction engine: a heavy tractor powered by a coal-fired steam engine

Tractor: in military terms, a prime mover for the relocation of artillery from one place to another

Transmission: the system of gears and propeller shafts used to take the power of the engine to the driving wheels or tracks

Trench lines: extensive and semi-permanent series of trenches designed to provide one side with deep enough defenses in sufficient depth to soak up the enemy's offensive strength without allowing him to penetrate into the rear areas

Index